www.blankbookbillionaire.com

CPSIA information can be obtained
at www.ICGtesting.com
Printed in the USA
BVHW041939180319
542996BV00015B/172/P

9 781981 731145